PMO Evaluations

Ronald N. Goulden, MBA, PMP

PMO Evaluations

Copyright © 2016

Ronald N. Goulden, MBA, PMP

ALL RIGHTS RESERVED

No portion of this publication may be reproduced, stored, or transmitted in any form, by any means, without written permission from the author.

Cover design by Ronald Goulden

ISBN: 978-1533098009

Table of Contents

Introduction 5
Macro Factors 9
    Planned Cost 9
    Actual Cost 10
    Cost Performance Index (CPI) 10
    Schedule Performance Index (SPI) 10
    Quality 10
Cost Performance Index (CPI) 10
Schedule Performance Index (SPI) 11
Quality Trend 12
Maturity Level 13
Operational Duration 14
PMO Rating 16
Micro Factors 19
    Corporate Goodwill 19
    It Goodwill 20
    PMO Leadership Experience 21
    PMO Maturity Level 22
    PM Maturity 23
    Executive Support 23
    Policeman and Auditors 25
    Burdensome Documentation 26
    Demand/Resource Management 27
    Benefits Capture 28
    PMO Leaders that don't know how to Adapt 29
    The PMO is a Project Manager's Nightmare 30
    No Strategic Vision 31
    Lack of a Metric-based Approach 32
    There is no PMO Charter 33
    The PMO is Rigid on Processes 33
    Does the PMO have a Plan 34
    Are the PMs Managing Projects or Reports 35
    Are Projects Prioritized 36
    Change Control Process 37
PMO Evaluation 38
Additional works by Ronald N. Goulden 42

Introduction

"It has been shown that deploying a PMO does not lead to performance improvement in itself. It is only when the PMO increases maturity that tangible improvement occurs." - ***Project Management - The State of the Industry - Center for Business Practices (CBP) Study***

Many times in their haste to implement a Project Management Office, the business leaders have a tendency to fail in placing adequate constraints on the PMO management, resulting in the implementation and enforcement of burdensome paperwork requirements.

Often, the fact that the business operations personnel really do not see the need for this tends to create a hostile and stressful relationship along with resistance from the business to what they perceive as bureaucratic nonsense.

The wise Project Management leaders will partner with the businesses and take great efforts to ensure the business is being adequately served.

In a time when analysts claim that the failure rate for PMOs is above fifty percent, we see executives hiring PMO leads from other companies, in many cases only to subsequently add their own failed PMO efforts to the statistical cemetery

In the eyes of the business leaders, the apparently 'logical' solution is to hire another displaced PMO leader and hope for a different result.

One must ask, "If the PMO lead was so effective, why is he or she available or searching for a new position?" There may be a legitimate answer, but this IS a question that MUST be asked.

It is apparent that there may be contributory factors leading to failed PMOs. The trick is to identify what those failure factors are and how to quantify their effects on the success or failure rates of these critical organizations. While some of these factors are patently obvious, others are more obscure.

If these 'failure' factors are identified and properly quantified; then a predictive model may be developed that will provide executives with a tool to identify PMO problems before they become costly, career-ending mistakes.

Typically, any PMO evaluation is based on the standard Project Management Metrics; Cost Performance Index (CPI) and Schedule Performance Index (SPI). As such, a form of Earned Value Management (EVM) is employed as part of the overall performance calculations. These can be called the Project Performance Macro Factors.

In addition to the CPI and SPI, a quantitative evaluation of the end product is required. Typically, most organizations do not have an effective quantitative tool for measuring project quality. An effective tool for measuring project Quality Performance is the Quality Scorecard.

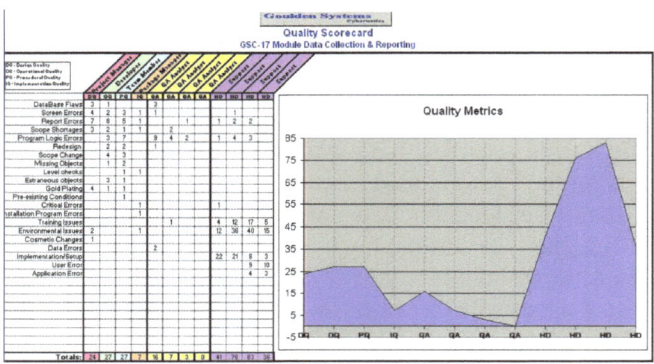

In the Performance graph supplied later in this document, the CPI, SPI, and Quality metrics have been factored along with the other metrics in order to provide a visual trend-line.

If an evaluation consisted merely of these three metrics, this report would provide little of a unique nature. An analysis of this nature can be performed with a simple spreadsheet,

In addition to the normal Macro Factors, an effective evaluation should include at the minimum, ten Micro Factors, which by their qualitative nature, typically are nor measured, reported, or even acknowledged by standard Project Management methodologies.

However, these Micro Factors have every bit as much of an impact on project and PMO performance as the more common Macro Factors.

When the aggregate Macro Factors are combined with the aggregate Micro Factors, patterns can be identified that help provide a forecast of PMO performance, based on historical activity and cultural proclivities.

Some of the PMO failures may actually be a function of the business culture, rather than simply a failure of the PMO leader.

Macro Factors

Historically, projects and subsequently the PMO have been evaluated on a small subset of available criteria. These are displayed on the following graph.

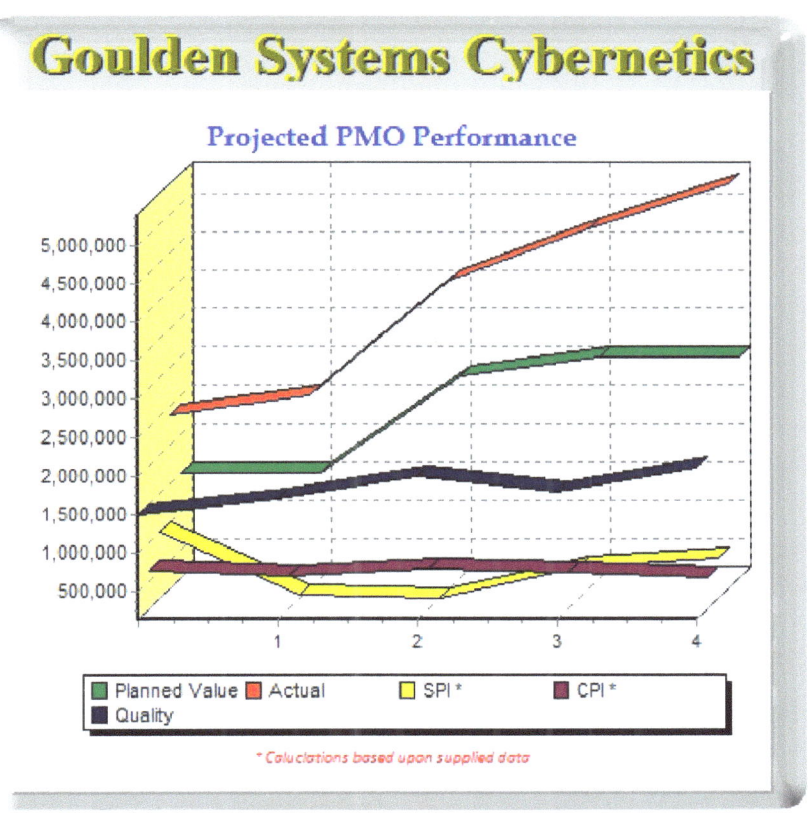

There are five measurable factors represented on the graph; Planned Cost (budget), Actual Cost, Schedule Performance Index (SPI), Cost Performance Index (CPI) and Quality. SPI, CPI, and Quality have been factored to display them on this graph for the purpose of illustrating trends and are not the actual values, which are much lower.

Planned Cost – The planned cost is the annual budget that is approved and set aside for project work and typically includes Capital and Expense components, as defined by your accounting department.

As business growth increases or expired facilities and systems reach 'end of life' it is normal for this value to grow at a steady rate. The expected slope of the budget is positive, upward and to the right.

Actual Cost – The actual cost represents the amount of money actually expended for project work. Normally, it is expected that this line will parallel the Planned Cost (budget), though (ideally) somewhat below.

If the Actual Cost is consistently or significantly above the Planned Cost, then the projects will display a historical trend of 'going over budget' and one would expect a negative CPI as a result.

When the Actual Cost exceeds the budget, the project is costing more than was planned; it is losing money. If the entire portfolio of projects exceeds the budget on a regular basis, then there are issues with task estimating, budgeting, and overall project management.

Cost Performance Index (CPI) – Normally, one would expect the CPI slope to be 'flat', or with a slight upward trend.

This would indicate a healthy budget management protocol.

A negative or wildly varying CPI indicates serious issues with budgeting and management. Money spent is difficult to recover. Poor CPI will affect other projects, having a negative, cascading effect on them.

Schedule Performance Index (SPI) – Like the Cost Performance Index, one would expect the SPI slope to be 'flat', or with a slight upward trend. As long as the SPI trend is positive, work is being completed on or ahead of schedule. When the SPI is negative or very erratic, this is an indication of problems with managing the project tasks, or poor task estimating.

'Scope Creep' can contribute to poor SPI performance. As new 'features' and undocumented enhancements are added to a project, the schedule will slip. Implementing good change management processes can control the negative effects of 'scope creep'.

Quality – One would expect the slope of a Quality trend line to be positive, consistently growing upward to the right. Ideally, this will become a flat line; however ensuring quality is a time-consuming effort requiring constant attention. Quality is the responsibility of everyone assigned to the project and must be approached in a participative team manner.

Cost Performance Index (CPI)

When the Cost Performance Index (CPI) trend is POSITIVE, that is, the CPI trend is greater than 1.0, the project pool has an earned value greater than the budget. This means that the project is performing effectively with respect to the budget. More work is being accomplished for the money than expected.

However, when the Cost Performance Index (CPI) trend is NEGATIVE, the aggregate CPI has a negative trend, it indicates a history of project cost overruns; requiring better budget controls.

If the CPI is less than 1.00, then less work is being completed per project dollar than planned. In other words, the projects are getting less than a dollar's value for each unit of work being completed.

A negative CPI means that the project is performing poorly with respect to the budget. Typically, once a project has a CPI below 1.0, it becomes very difficult to 'make up' or recover those costs.

The typical 'knee-jerk' reaction is to throw more resources at the project to get it back on track (this is called 'crashing'). If project crashing is undertaken, the Project Manager must understand how to obtain maximum duration compression with the minimal cost.

A Cost Performance Index (CPI) of less than 1.00 represents a critical concern, and possibly one that is irrecoverable.

Crashing will always have an adverse effect on the budget and the Cost Performance Index (CPI).

Again, be aware that a poor CPI is extremely difficult to correct.

Schedule Performance Index (SPI)

The Schedule Performance Index (SPI) provides an objective indication of the performance of any project with respect to its schedule. When the SPI trend is POSITIVE, greater than or equal to 1.0, the project pool has taken less time to complete tasks than expected. This means that the projects are performing well with respect to the schedule.

This generally indicates good project management practices and strong control of the project resources.

When the Schedule Performance Index (SPI) trend is NEGATIVE, or the aggregate SPI has a negative trend, it indicates a history of project schedule issues, resulting in delayed project delivery; requiring better task estimation and task monitoring.

Since the Schedule Performance Index (SPI) provides an objective indication of the performance of any project with respect to its schedule. When the SPI trend is NEGATIVE, less than 1.0, then the project tasks have taken more time to complete than expected. This means that the projects are performing poorly with respect to the schedule.

This generally indicates poor Project Management practices and weak control of the project resources. The level of effort estimates may have been understated, or the overall scope of the projects may not have been accurately defined.

However, project schedule problems can be caused by external sources. Executive Management may have mandated an unreasonable time constraint, or deadline, resulting in an abbreviated schedule that is unreasonable and unattainable. The Project Manager and PMO may have had their recommendations to resolve these issues rejected.

Schedule performance can generally be corrected if the issue is detected early enough.

Quality Trend

When the Quality trend is POSITIVE, this generally indicates the user community is satisfied with the results of the projects; the timeliness of their delivery and associated costs.

However, quality is something that can ALWAYS be improved. Use a tool like the Quality Scorecard to closely monitor project quality during project execution, rather than waiting for the users to determine the projects' quality.

If the Quality trend is NEGATIVE, and the aggregate Quality has a negative trend, it indicates a history of project deliveries that fail to meet the users' needs, are delivered behind schedule, or exceed budget requirements.

Determining overall quality is a difficult task because there are so many quantitative factors and qualitative factors that the users will employ to determine the overall project satisfaction.

A Negative Quality trend indicates that the users (customers) are NOT satisfied with the results of the projects.

This may be a result of the projects not providing the expected or desired results; or the projects were delivered so far behind schedule or over budget to be of little value to the customer.

Again, employing a tool such as the Quality Scorecard can provide a better 'finger on the quality pulse' of the projects, providing early indications of quality issues, rather waiting until the customer has taken possession of the project before discovering significant quality issues.

It is important to engage the Quality Assurance team early in the project lifecycles so that they become aware to the scope and objectives of the projects.

If the Quality teams understand the projects, they will be able to perform more precise testing and validation. By working with the Quality team, the project resources can 'build quality into the project' rather than trying to 'bolt on' quality afterwards.

Maturity Level

Much like humans, PMO Maturity Level indicates how the Project Management function relates to the accepted rules and processes and how to function effectively with others.

For the sake of calculations and evaluations, five levels of maturity are employed when reviewing PMOs. Level One is the lowest, most immature with Level Five being the most mature and, presumably, the most effective.

PMO Maturity Level One:

A Level One PMO is immature, with less than 25% successful project completion. There will be a significant degree of variation among project management and delivery. There will be numerous 'stealth' projects and significant gold-plating and 'scope creep'.

At this level, there is a tremendous amount of room for improvement and the PMO leadership must have a clear vision and the skill to mold plans and ideals to meet the needs of reality. Any ambiguity or indecisiveness in PMO leadership will cause failure.

At Maturity Level One, there is a very high probability for project failure.

PMO Maturity level Two:

With a Level Two maturity, the PMO is established, but is likely to be in great need of improvement.

Successful project completion rates of 35 to 35% are typical for this maturity level. Some project management tools will become standardized.

Typically the SPI and CPI will be below 1.0 frequently and Customer-Satisfaction will average around 50%. As a general rule, more project still fail than succeed.

There is a good probability of PMO failure unless the PMO leadership enforces the use of EVM and good time management skills.

PMO Maturity level Three:

At Maturity Level Three, the PMO can be considered Grown Up, and probably has more successes than failures. Many management tools will be standardized and some reporting will be consolidated.

However, there is still a possibility of PMO failure unless the leadership maintains its vision and maturity.

At Level Three, the PMO can be considered to be on the cusps of success or failure.

PMO Maturity level Four:

At Level Four, the PMO is mature and more than likely, very successful. At this level it is expected that 90% of projects will complete on-time, under-budget, and with high levels of customer-satisfaction. The SPI and CPI should typically be above 1.0, with rare exceptions.

Many standardized tools and processes will be in place with generally accepted understanding of how to use those tools and processes.

PMO Maturity level Five:

A level five PMO can be considered 'Best in Class'.

It is expected that 99% of projects complete on-time, under-budget, and with very high levels of customer-satisfaction.

At this level, the Business and IT Communities view the PMO as an important partner that brings unquestioned value to the Business.

While there may still be room for improvement, the PMO should focus on maintaining consistency and meeting the continued high expectations of the Business.

At this level, there should be the maximum focus on continuous quality and process improvement.

Operational Duration

Process change takes time; and implementing, or 'fixing', a PMO is a Process Improvement.

For the sake of calculations and evaluations, five years of operations are employed when reviewing PMOs. Year One is the lowest, least experienced with Year Five being the most experienced and, presumably, the most effective.

When the PMO is in its First year:

With a year or less of operational experience, the PMO is Immature. A PMO that has been in operation for a year or less has barely had time to perform a needs assessment or GAP analysis. At best, the organization will be in the planning and design stage during the first year.

Successful project completion and reporting will frequently be below 25%.

Being inexperienced, the PMO has a great deal of work to do to gain any viability. The PMO leadership must be able to articulate a clear vision and possess the flexibility to adjust plans and ideals to meet the needs of reality. There is a tremendous amount of room for improvement.

When the PMO is in its Second year:

In the Second Year, while the PMO may be established, it will be in dire need of improvement. Original plans and processes may have to be scrapped and rebuilt to meet the needs of the business and coexist within the culture of the company.

While successful project completion may be in the 30 to 35% range. This implies that there are still considerable slippages with respect to Budget, Schedule, and Quality. Much of the performance improvement may be more the result of the Project Managers learning from their mistakes than from any operational efficiencies provided by the PMO at this time.

There is significant room for improvement.

When the PMO is in its Third year:

At three years, the PMO should be considered Grown Up, having more successes than failures. Many processes and tools will have been implemented and the Project teams will have developed a level of comfort with these tools and processes.

Sixty percent of projects should complete on-tine, under-budget, with acceptable levels of user-satisfaction.

There is still a great deal of room for improvement.

PMO success or failure now hinges on the management skills of the PMO leader. If Project performance is still below the expectations of the business, then the PMO leader must be able to articulate the reasons for the deficiencies and present and defend the PMO plan moving into the future; reiterating that the PMO is barely halfway through its implementation cycle.

When the PMO is in its Fourth year:

At four years, the PMO should be effective and very successful, with more than 90% of the projects completing on-time, under-budget, and with high levels of user-satisfaction.

The Schedule Performance Index and the Cost performance Index should be consistently at or above 1.0. The project quality and customer-satisfaction should generally be very good.

At four years, any unnecessary processes and tools have been eliminated or replaced and the project teams fully understand their roles and goals. The Project teams should have a sense of pride in their accomplishments.

<u>When the PMO is in its Fifth year:</u>

As such, one would expect it to be 'Best in Class" with less than 0.7% project issues. The CPI and SPI should consistently be above 1.0 and the Quality score should be at 100%.

By the fifth year, the PMO leader has provided a tremendous value to the business. However, the benefits must be continually proselytized and improvements must be continuously implemented. It is incumbent upon the PMO Leader to be the 'Press Agent' for the organization to ensure that the business recognizes the accomplishments and achievements of the PMO.

PMO Rating

The PMO rating is a function of how the business views the PMO organization and the Project Management function. For the sake of simplicity, I utilize a Poor, Average, and Good rating that suffices for evaluation purposes. There is nothing to be gained by trying to become more granular than these three classifications.

The ratings are the responsibility of all members of the PMO, including the Project Managers and the individual team members,

<u>If the PMO rating is POOR:</u>

If the PMO rating is POOR, then the PMO is not performing to the expectations of the business.

In all fairness, the PMO may be in a 'start-up' mode and the resulting immaturity reflects in poor performance.

With this rating, there is tremendous room for improvement as well as great potential for failure.

It is essential that Earned Value Management be implemented and the PMO Leadership provide the guidance and support to the Project Managers to ensure they can help the PMO grow.

With a POOR rating, there are only two directions the PMO can go; upward by improving, or 'out the door' by failing to improve.

PMO rating is AVERAGE:

With an AVERAGE rating, the PMO can be considered to be grown up, with more successes than failures. However, it is far from being 'best of class'. There is significant room for improvement and growth.

AVERAGE is just that, mediocre. While there may be successes and visible improvements, it would be foolish to become lax and settle for this rating.

Remember, this rating is how the corporate peers view the PMO and its leadership and team members. An AVERAGE rating will not win any awards or positive recognition. The best anyone could say about the PMO is that 'it could be worse'.

Average indicates that there is significant room for growth or decline; complacency will result in failure.

PMO rating is GOOD:

If the business rates the PMO as Good, then the PMO is grown up, consistently having more successes than failures. In many respects, it is considered to be mature and very successful. However, it may not be a 'world class' organization.

Remember that there is ALWAYS room for improvement. Retaining a GOOD rating is a constant struggle for process improvements and innovation.

Having a GOOD rating is not cause to celebrate and 'rest on your laurels'; it means that the PMO is operating at expected levels of efficiency and success. Remember that GOOD is merely 'good enough'.

Micro Factors

The Micro Factors are those characteristics that are often difficult to quantify, but certainly have a qualitative effect on the success of a PMO (or any other) organization.

The data used as inputs for the Micro Factor calculations is typically provided by the Executive Committee or the functional managers. It should NEVER be provided by the PMO Organization.

The reason for having the customers (the Executive Committee and Functional Managers) provide inputs with respect to the Micro Factors is to provide objectivity. Later, when the performance rating graphic is provided, any challenges to the graphic can be defused by simply providing the caveat that the data for the graphic was provided by the users (the Executive Committee and Functional Managers), and is representative of their opinions and viewpoints.

Corporate Goodwill

Corporate Goodwill will almost always mimic the PMO Rating discussed earlier.

It is essential that the PMO and its personnel have a good relationship with all levels of the business. Overbearing and dictatorial personalities will destroy any chances of a successful PMO implementation.

While the PMO is an agent of change for the organization, the transformation must be evolutionary rather than revolutionary.

If the PMO ostracizes the business community by rapidly implementing onerous policies and process that appear to hinder rather than help the company, the normal levels of resistance to change will increase dramatically, resulting in a dramatic and 'inexplicable' failure for the PMO Leader.

Too often, a 'new' PMO leader will implement new processes and policies (possibly carried over from a PMO implementation at a previous company) expecting the business to 'fall in line' and embrace the changes. The problem with this is that something that worked at one company may fail horribly as a new company.

** Correction **

The PMO leaders and staff must ensure that they take great efforts to work within the scope and needs of the business community they serve. The PMO must help facilitate change, not mandate change. The Project Managers and Business Analysts must work as partners with the business, guiding when necessary and suggesting relevant opportunities for improvement, without appearing overbearing.

Do not speak jargon, or 'techno-babble' to the business; speak the language of your hosts, the business leaders.

The PMO must always remember that it is a service organization, not the driving force behind the overall business operations. The PMO serves at the pleasure of the Executive Committee.

In many cases, the PMO leaders should listen more and talk less. When the PMO leader is talking, he or she is not listening to the business and the business is not talking. A successful PMO requires two-way discourse.

It Goodwill

Many projects are Information Technology (IT) projects and as such require the active involvement and cooperative participation of the IT personnel. A hostile IT Department can passively bring a PMO to its knees while having the appearance of absolute cooperation.

Even if a project is purely business-oriented, there is a high probability that IT resources or services will be necessary to achieve success. A PMO cannot survive or prosper without IT Goodwill.

That being said, the IT Goodwill sword is truly double-edged. The IT Functions must have goodwill toward the PMO and the business must have a strong sense of goodwill toward the technology departments.

In many businesses, events may have transpired to cause the IT department to be viewed less than favorably by the business leaders. The IT and PMO leaders must work cooperatively in order to succeed.

If the PMO is guiding an IT effort in an environment where technology is viewed with disdain, the chances of a successful project implementation will be daunting. It is in the best interests of IT and the PMO to develop a nurturing relationship.

** Correction **

The PMO leaders and staff must ensure that they take great efforts to work with the IT community. Again, the PMO must remember that it is a service organization and not the driving force behind the business operations.

In many cases, the IT department should be viewed as a critical success factor for the projects managed by the PMO. At the very least, a hostile IT department can be classified as a constraint or even a risk.

In many cases, the PMO leaders need to listen more than talk. When the PMO leader is talking, he or she is not listening to the business and the business is not talking. The PMO leader must not disregard the IT department or take it for granted.
-A successful PMO requires teamwork at all levels.

PMO Leadership Experience

As with any leadership role, a critical success factor for a PMO is directly related to the experience and maturity level of the PMO leadership.

All too often, a 'leader' is recruited from outside of the organization to implement a PMO. The question that must be asked of the leadership team is "Why is that PMO leader available? If the external candidate is so spectacular, why exactly is he or she on the market?"

Remember that an external candidate may not have a thorough understanding of your particular business operation or even the culture of the company. While determining the fit of an external candidate is ultimately the responsibility of the hiring official, a poor fit will result in widespread damage.

Sometimes recruiting an outside PMO leader will be ineffective because you may find yourself hiring someone else's mistakes. There may be instances where the new PMO leader acts like a fledgling PMP and tries to implement every policy and practice found in a book or gathered from a seminar.

** Correction **

The wise PMO leader will assess the business and will be able to adjust the design and implementation schedule of the PMO policies and processes to comply with the realities of the business.

A poorly implemented PMO can cause chaos with the day to day operations of the business. The PMO leadership MUST have excellent Organizational Awareness.

That being said, it is critical that the PMO have a published Charter and implementation plan. Remember that establishing a PMO is actually a project of itself.

PMO Maturity Level

As with project managers, a Project Management Office typically tends to get better with age and experience. The PMO leadership and team must learn from their mistakes and be adaptable, to accommodate the needs of the business.

A new PMO has a lot of ground to cover and a great deal of work before it becomes marginally effective. Attempts to 'rush' the implementation of the PMO processes may have an adverse effect on project productivity.

-Do not expect tremendous returns from a PMO in the first or second year. The organizationally immature team will make mistakes and poor decisions.

Remember that PMO's and project managers are actually people with set agendas and personal propensities. It takes time to train and educate the new team on how the PMO procedures work and what the benefits are.

The breakdown of PMO Maturity across all surveyed organizations is as follows:

Level 1 - Immature: 25.7%
Level 2 - Established, in need of improvement: 34.4%
Level 3 - Grown up, more successes than failures: 30.4%
Level 4 - Mature, very successful: 8.7%
Level 5 - Best in class: 0.7%

The State of the PMO - 2007-2008 - A Benchmark of Current Business Practices (Center for Business Practices (CBP) Report)

As you can see from these statistics, more than sixty percent of PMO organizations are functionally immature.

** Correction **

Be sure to have a clearly defined PMO implementation plan with well-defined milestones and critical dates. Manage the expectations of the business so that it is understood that building an effective PMO is an on-going work in progress.

If the PMO Leader is a true leader, he or she should have a five-year plan for the PMO, outlining growth goals with measurable milestones and objectives.

Part of this five-year plan should clearly express how the team will grow and what will be necessary to achieve that growth.

PM Maturity

One of the most common mistakes a new Project Manager makes is to try to implement the Project Management Body of Knowledge (PMBOK) company-wide. That does not work. The PMI model is not a 'one-size fits all'; it is a general guideline to be tailored to specific needs. However, in their zeal, the newly anointed PMP will try to restructure the business processes overnight.

Typically, the beginning Project Manager will create a lot of unnecessary work and stress before finally learning what works best for each business. With time and experience, greater efficiencies will be realized.

"In low-performing organizations, PMO staff are much less likely to have formal project management qualifications, hands-on-experience and extensive project management knowledge." -T*he State of the PMO - 2007-2008 - A Benchmark of Current Business Practices (Center for Business Practices (CBP) Report)*

This is not to imply that uncertified Project Managers are inferior to PMPs. This indicates that sometimes experiential knowledge needs augmentation with the addition of more formalized processes and tools.

** Correction **

An effective PMO can throttle some of the enthusiasm of the novice PMPs and guide them along a path that meets the needs of the business. Like the PMO, Project Managers are works in progress. Even experienced Project Managers must learn and adapt to any new policies or processes.

With time, Project Managers will adapt to what works best for the business and fulfills the needs of the PMO. Remember that there is no 'one size fits all' in the realm of Project Management or the PMO.

The PMO Leader must grow and nurture the Project Manager to fulfill the needs of the business. In cases where a Project Manager refuses to learn, then that calls for a reassignment.

Executive Support

Normally, when the Executive team realizes there's a problem with projects not executing properly, contending for too few resources, or just not delivering results, their response is to authorize a PMO, with the expectation that the new PMO will automatically and instantaneously solve the problems.

All too often, the Executives find themselves too busy or disinterested to attend the steering committee meetings and make the necessary hard decisions.

As a result they may delegate attendance to lower-level staff members without authorizing them the corresponding decision-making authority.

Then, when projects are once again performing poorly due to resource contention and prioritization conflicts, they blame the PMO and either disband it or micromanage it.

There are many reasons for the lack of executive support and it manifests in many forms. There may be the public chiding, the noticeable loss of respect within the 'inner circle'.

Discussions may occur around making 'no additional changes for the foreseeable future' at a given point in time (even though the only change may have been the implementation of a project dashboard).

Another failure tactic is to display the apparent inability to comprehend key concepts even after multiple explanations - like the PM life-cycle; Management may be sending a message that they see the PMO as ineffective.

Another classic tendency is to cut funding support, new positions are denied or existing positions are reduced. Those experiencing it recognize it as a lack of Executive support, and this will always 'end' a PMO. At best, the PMO will be relegated to 'other duties as assigned'.

Many times (most times I would imagine) an organization's management will fixate on the idea that a PMO is necessary to make things better, then hire or promote some key people, and wait for 'the better'.

This is a tremendous opportunity for a project professional; but running a PMO is not the same as running a project. And, if you run projects as a glorified administrative assistant; documenting tasks, taking and sending out meeting notes, preparing RED-YELLOW-GREEN reports and not as a true project leader and an excellent communicator throughout the organization, you'll find support erodes quickly.

** Correction **

If there is no Executive support for your PMO, it's because the PMO leader has not delivered a compelling reason for the PMO group's existence and/or has not delivered the value promised. (And, an implicit promise was made to add value to the organization the moment the position was accepted.)

Whether the types of value to be created, or the manner in which value would be created were specifically defined is irrelevant. Remember, at some level, someone specified the value the PMO team would create, either explicitly or implicitly.

It is critical that the PMO have an approved Charter and a clearly defined Project Plan. Similarly, it is essential that the Executive Committee and the PMO have a precise understanding of the value to be delivered by the PMO and when the deliverables are due.

The PMO five-year plan is a critical tool for the viability of the PMO.

Policeman and Auditors

One purpose of a PMO is to bring value to the Project Managers, so auditing and policing for a bit is to be expected in an educational and mentoring manner. It helps drive the change through change-resistant organizations.

However, if the PMO has functioned in this mode for more than a year, then its perceived role will differ dramatically from what its Charter should be.

The PMO may become a bureaucratic process that is cumbersome and overbearing while providing little value to the business.

If more time is spent auditing the Project Managers than is employed in driving projects toward success, PMO failure is likely. The PMO leader should not be functioning as the 'Chief of Police' or an auditor as a full-time task,

** Correction **

While start-up PMOs do require more 'hands on' monitoring of the Project Managers than a more mature organization, that role should exist as a relative low percentage of the PMO Leader's bandwidth and awareness.

Remember that the primary goal of the PMO is to provide better functioning Project Management and project completion.

Avoid the tendency to over-audit or over-control.

Remember that each project is unique with distinct requirements; not every project will require the same level of scrutiny and control. Some Project Managers will be more effective than others.

Be realistic in the process and audit mechanism. A forty hour project does not need the same level of scrutiny as a four thousand hour project. Different categories of projects must be held to different standards.

Do NOT bring a project to a halt because a particular check-point was missed in the past. Keep the projects moving forward; do not allow documentation to halt project execution. Doing so will invite project failure at the expense of the PMO's documentation standards record.

Treat documentation deficiencies as part of the 'Lessons Learned'. Every misstep should be viewed as a 'teaching moment'.

Burdensome Documentation

People drive project success. Processes and technology should improve effectiveness, not become obstacles.

Additionally PMO processes should aid in the PMO organization as a communication tool and for goals alignment improvement.

As an example, Risk Management is a great process for identifying possible obstacles and potential issues for the project. However if they aren't communicated to those accountable and empowered for managing the risk, the process is just more documentation for the already overburdened PM.

Do not require a specific form of Project documentation unless it is really necessary and required. Just because a PMO Leader places a document on a checklist that should not mean that that document is required for every project, even if its use makes absolutely no sense.

Too often, PMO leadership become enamored with its forms and templates, requiring the Project Managers to complete documentation that adds minimal value or is hopelessly redundant. There are instances where Project Managers have been forced to repeatedly update or modify existing forms as the PMO Leadership refines and redesigns those documents.

Remember that the primary function of a Project Manager is to manage projects and not to be a testing ground for PMO documentation.

** Correction **

Do not allow documentation to halt project execution. While it is nice for the PMO leader to state that all projects are 100% up-to-date on required documentation and all PMO processes have been followed, value is lost if all of the projects are behind schedule and over budget, or deliver a product that is completely useless to the user.

Be aware that any artificial delay injected into the Project flow will affect the cost, schedule, or quality of the project. A new reporting metric devised by the PMO leader may take the Project Manager's time from managing the project, while providing little actual information of any value. (In many cases, the PMO Leader could complete some of the forms for the Project Managers.)

Always balance the need for documentation against the needs of the project. If a new process or new report or project artifact hinders the effective completion of the project, the process or artifact must be reconsidered and possibly discarded.

Do NOT require Project Managers to 'retro-fit' new documentation to existing projects. This is a complete waste of time and adds absolutely no value to the existing project.

Demand/Resource Management

The project pipeline, or backlog, is a basic Project Management requirement, and its management is a critical success factor for the PMO.

If the PMO leader cannot quantify demand, and the Project Managers find that their priorities change all day long; it will be impossible to forecast needs and resource availability.

Also if there are no available resources for the projects, Project Manager heroics only goes so far, and the projects will not be accomplished. Do not expect a Project Manager to constantly work horrendous hours to save a project. Ensuring that the proper resources are in place to meet the demands of the business with respect to the project Pipeline. If Project Managers are working extended hours, the PMO Leader has not executed proper resource planning.

The PMO controls the project pipeline as well as negotiations for resources.

However, in many instances the PMO allocates resources at 100% utilization. This is foolish and displays lack of understanding of the resource pool. No one can work 100% on any project; there are meetings, phone calls, illnesses, and other interruptions.

Specialized resources may have only small windows of opportunity available for each project. A delay in one project can negatively affect all other 'downstream' projects.

A haphazard approach to project demand makes it impossible to determine necessary resources and timing. If the Executive Committee is not informed otherwise, they may assume that every project will be assigned and completed on time and under budget.

** Correction **

Accurate tracking of project time is critical. If necessary, the PMO can help assist developing a process for time tracking while remaining aware of the Work Interruption Factor (WIF) for each available resource.

The Work Interruption Factor (WIF) will be different for every resource. Many PMO Leaders are unable to understand why their most experienced resource often misses deadlines or has to work extra hours.

Keep in mind that the experienced resource is very likely a Subject Matter Expert (SME) and is called upon to answer questions from less experienced team members, or even attend meetings with the Project Managers or PMO Leader, all of which dramatically increase the Work Interruption Factor.

The Project Managers must communicate any schedule or resource issues to the PMO immediately. Ultimately, it is the responsibility of the PMO Leader to ensure that all projects have the resources necessary to successfully complete the projects.

PMO Leadership must fairly and accurately represent resource availability and scheduling, with modifications as necessary. Failure to keep the Executive team apprised of resource shortfalls will result in project and PMO failures.

Normally, there is a finite number of resources that can be scheduled. As conflicting demands for projects arise, the PMO must negotiate with the Executive team regarding which projects have priority and can use existing resource pools, which projects will require authorization for contract resources, and which projects will be deferred.

An 'above the bar - below the bar' approach may be necessary to communicate which projects are in the active pipeline and which ones are being deferred, due to resource or budget shortfalls.

Benefits Capture

One universal issue it how to continue to facilitate and drive value through the PMO processes. This requires a bit of marketing, but is generally well worth the time spent.

The PMO should help to capture and quantify the business value of the completed projects. If the PMO Leadership does not capture the benefits, it is more than likely they will not be captured.

Ultimately, the organization will ask, "What is the value in the PMO overhead?" Being proactive mitigates this argument altogether. If the PMO cannot advertise the benefit it bring to the organization, then the PMO will fail.

PMO Leadership should be able to explain the value provided by the PMO at any time and for any audience. The Wise PMO Leader will have these 'talking points' available at all times.

Too often, the PMO will focus on budget and schedule metrics, since they are easiest to quantify and explain or put on a graph. Typically, there is no attempt at quantifying the quality metrics for the projects, or even the micro factors.

Normally, the user measures project success by how well the project meets their needs. The average user is not concerned with budget or schedule issues.

** Correction **

To successfully capture the Benefits of the project, the PMO MUST implement Earned Value Management (EVM), accompanied with a realistic measure of the quality of the project deliverables, typically expressed as Customer Satisfaction. The Quality Scorecard is an excellent tool for measuring project deliverable quality and customer satisfaction.

Without EVM and Quality Metrics, the PMO is merely 'guessing' at the benefits provided by the project.

Do not force the business owners to determine the benefits of completed projects. The PMO should measure and report while the business confirms and validates those benefits. The PMO Leadership has all of the information necessary to quantify the benefits of the PMO, and, with a little work, can quantify Quality and the micro factors.

PMO Leaders that don't know how to Adapt

What worked in one company most likely won't work in another, despite similarities on paper. (Actually the proper statement is "What worked at one company will NOT work in a new company without modification.)

If a PMO leader isn't adaptable and tries a 'cookie cutter' approach based on experience from a prior employer, then the PMO is likely to fail. Things like slight variations in the business model and corporate culture can have a devastating effect on a 'cookie cutter PMO'.

Many times, a PMO Leader may leave a successful PMO implementation at one company and expect the same formula to work in a new company. The new PMO leader may have a 'flawed' expectation that the new company will learn to adapt.

While implementing a PMO is an evolutionary process, the adaptation of the company must be matched with the adaptability of the PMO Leadership.

Businesses are different, even within the same industry. Each organization has its own culture and personality. Business models have subtle variations.

A better approach is to understand the unique drivers and pain points for the organization, the various personalities and motivations of key stakeholders, and determine whether the culture of the organization supports the ability to develop a plan with achievable goals.

** Correction **

Do not bring past mistakes into a new or struggling PMO. Understand the business and its needs and drivers. Organizational culture varies widely. What worked (or partially worked) in one organization may fail miserably in another. (It is highly possible that what 'worked' at the previous company only partially worked.)

Be flexible and innovative.

Partner with the business to forge a PMO that will exceed their expectations. If the business is involved in the PMO design and implementation, the chances of success will increase greatly.

In order to effect change and improvement, the PMO Leadership must be willing to adapt to the needs of the company.

The PMO is a Project Manager's Nightmare

In many ways a PMO director has to be part cheerleader, part salesperson and part coach, making sure that the PMO's mission/charter is well articulated and all stakeholders buy into it.

However, if a PMO becomes part auditor and mostly methodology police, forcing adoption of ill-fitting methodologies or gathering unnecessary information, it will become a hindrance to Project Managers and rejected by the organization.

Often, the PMO Leadership expects to shift its reporting burden to the Project Managers; even forcing the Project Managers to develop slides for inclusion in the PMO presentation deck for the Executives.

There instances where the PMO Leadership expected the Project Managers to develop PMO documentation, artifacts, and processes for the PMO. The result was that the Project Managers spent all of their time trying to meet the demands of the PMO Leader rather than managing the projects. (Of course the PMO Leader became enraged when he had to tell the Executive Committee that all of the projects were behind schedule and over budget.)

The PMO may demand that all projects, regardless of status, be maintained at the same level of documentation, even as new documents and artifacts are developed and implemented.

Requiring the Project Managers to do the work of the PMO Leadership WILL cause the Project Managers to fail.

** Correction **

Remember that the job of a Project Manager is to manage projects. If the PMO micro-manages the Project Managers, the projects will suffer. The Project Managers will focus more on meeting the demands of the PMO than on guiding the projects to successful completion.

Streamline reporting and documentation to the bare minimum required for the Project Managers to effectively report project progress and status.

Remember that it is the responsibility of the PMO to report to the Executives, not the individual Project Managers. While the Project Managers can provide input to the presentation deck for the Executives, the PMO is responsible for standardizing the presentation and performing the necessary interpretations and extrapolations.

The PMO Leader is completely responsible for what is presented to the Executive Committee. It is in the best interest of the PMO Leader to develop his or her own presentations, only reaching out to the Project Managers for specific informational elements that they alone would have knowledge of.

Again, do NOT expect or demand that the Project Managers spend several hours a week developing slides and documents for an Executive briefing deck; that is the responsibility of the PMO.

No Strategic Vision

Focusing on tactical, day-to-day execution is fine, but the PMO Leadership and teams need to not lose sight of the bigger, strategic picture. The PMO must provide a strategic plan for how the company will effectively manage projects. Typically, this will be a three or five year plan, sometimes expressed as a roadmap.

If a PMO leader can't grasp and articulate the business challenges faced by senior executives, and help facilitate organizational change and alignment to meet those challenges, the PMO will become less relevant to an organization.

For all practical purposes, establishing and running an effective PMO is a project that requires a formal plan. The PMO project plan is part of the strategic planning that is absolutely the responsibility of the PMO Leadership.

The PMO Leader is the de facto 'head of state' for the company's project management efforts. If the leader has no published plan, the PMO Leader may appear as a 'cowboy' or completely 'clueless'.

** Correction **

The PMO Project Plan (PMOPP) is a document that is published and maintained. Its activity should be reported to the Executive Committee regularly.

Minimally, the plan should be revised each year to reflect changes to business needs or current trends or legislation. In a more dynamic environment, the updates may occur quarterly; but never more frequently.

Without a PMOPP, there is no strategy and the PMO leadership is failing their duty to the business. If the Project Managers require a plan to execute the business projects, then the PMO Leader needs a plan to execute the business project to implement and maintain a PMO.

The PMO Leadership should allow the Project Manager to focus on the tactical, day-to-day issues so that the PMO can focus on the longer range requirements of the business.

Lack of a Metric-based Approach

Unless a PMO leader has an analytical mindset and is comfortable with metrics, a PMO will not be successful. A PMO may be functioning wonderfully, but if that performance cannot be readily demonstrated and articulate, the PMO is a failure.

For example, when it comes to deciding how many of the top projects can actually be done, the decision process too often turns to pure guess work. Without a metrics-based understanding of resource capacity, it is impossible to match demand with the actual supply of human resources.

EVM can provide an accurate barometer of the status of each project with respect to cost and schedule. Poorly functioning project may be deferred, or 'dropped below the line' to allow more viable projects to consume valuable resources.

Most Project Managers and PMO Leaders do not understand Earned Value Management (EVM). Since they do not understand, EVM is not implemented, despite the value it brings to Project Management.

While EVM can provide metrics for budget and schedule performance, capturing quality performance and the micro factors becomes a bit more difficult.

** Correction **

The PMO Leadership should implement a Project time tracking system and enforce the use of Earned Value Management. This may require some training on the part of the PMO Leadership and the Project Managers.

Implement a tool like the Quality Scorecard to track and measure project quality performance.

Most Project Management programs provide some level of Earned Value Management functionality. Implementing EVM at the Project level should not be too difficult a task.

However, the PMO should be able to provide aggregate EVM metrics by project Manager, business unit, and line of business. This can provide valuable insights into how well the PMO is meeting its goals.

There is no PMO Charter

Without a Charter, the PMO will be ineffectual and possibly be perceived as arbitrary and capricious. The Charter is the document that provides the PMO Leadership with the authority to execute.

Often, the purpose and objectives of the PMO are loosely implied or poorly stated. Without clear articulation of the goals and objectives of the PMO, there is a strong likelihood that the Executive Committee and the PMO Leadership will become 'conflicted' over the performance of the PMO. Ultimately, the inept PMO Leader will blame the Executives for not supporting the PMO effort.

The PMO organization needs a clear description of its purpose and its responsibilities for project teams, executive teams, and individuals in the organization. This can be a simple value statement or it can be an elevator pitch, or it can be a bullet list description on the organization's intranet. It needs to be quick, easy to grasp, and easy to remember.

** Correction **

Make sure the PMO Charter is clear, concise, and unambiguous. DO not leave any room for confusion about the PMO organization and its goals and objectives. Make sure the Charter is readily available to everyone in the organization (post it on the Company Intranet).

The Charter should also define the responsibilities and authorities of the PMO and how it fits within the organizational structure of the company.

Since the PMO will use company resources, the PMO Charter must be signed by a company officer.

The PMO is Rigid on Processes

For the PMO organization, process is very important. However, if a process is too rigid and inflexible, the PMO will fail. Review process and documentation requirements and ensure that they are appropriate for the needs of the business.

There have been instances where the Project Managers have been required to provide 40 hours of documentation for a 20 hour project. The PMO failed to ensure that the level of effort required for its processes was appropriate for the size of the projects.

Remember that process is nothing more than a guide or a model; it should not be a burdensome mandate.

PMO Organizations sometimes spend an inordinate amount of time defining, documenting, training, and explaining processes when the project team becomes stalled, without really solving the problem.

All of these can help to a point, and after that they force the organization down a narrow path rather than freeing the teams to think creatively.

The ultimate goal of a PMO is to create value for the customer, not merely to define a rigid set of instructions that will throttle productivity.

** Correction **

Processes, artifacts and controls are important as long as they do not become a 'road-block' to productivity and stifle innovation; they must have relevance and provide value.

It is incumbent upon the PMO Leadership to ensure that any process, document, or artifact is appropriate for the type or size of project being worked.

The process for obtaining an exception from the process must be clear and concise and absolutely unambiguous and understandable. (Be aware that regardless of how well the exception rules are defines, someone WILL make a mistake.)

Be flexible. The ultimate measure of the success of the PMO Organization is not in its documentation or processes, but in results (Budget, Schedule, and Quality).

Does the PMO have a Plan

How can a PMO manage Project Manager and Projects if it cannot even develop a plan for itself?

Again, all too often, a PMO Organization 'sets up office' and begins issuing policy and processes without any clearly defined plan of action. This 'ad hoc' management of the PMO Organization is a critical factor for failure.

Remember that the PMO cannot lead Project Management teams if it cannot develop and execute a plan for its own implementation and operation.

Many times, Executives sanction a PMO Organization, expecting it to be a 'magic wand' that will make all of the Project Management problems go away. Only after a few years into the PMO effort does it become apparent that the PMO Organization is failing, or the Executives realize they have no idea what the PMO Organization has done or plans to do.

** Correction **

Along with having a Charter, the PMO should have a formal project plan for implementation. This should be a three to five year plan with milestones, deliverables and critical dates. The PMO project plan should be reported in the same manner as any other project.

The wise PMO Leader will develop the PMO Project Plan (PMOPP) and present it to the Executive Committee for review and approval. By providing a roadmap of how the PMO will correct Project Management issues, along with deliverables and timelines, the expectations of the Executives can be more clearly defined and managed.

Each year, the PMOPP should be reviewed, adjusted, and approved by the Executive Committee. This will help the PMO Leader ensure that the PMO Organization is properly aligned with the needs and goals of the business.

Are the PMs Managing Projects or Reports

As the pressure to deliver builds on the PMO Organization, that pressure is typically distributed downward to the Project Managers.

Many times, the Project Managers find themselves spending an inordinate amount of time developing reports for presentation to the Executives for the PMI Leader. Time spent on developing Executive-level reports is time that is taken away from actually managing the projects.

Many PMO Leaders 'delegate' report preparation to the Project Managers. While Project Managers are responsible for reporting status, condition, and progress of their projects, only a lazy PMO Leader expects the Project Managers to prepare slides for the PMO Leader to present to the Executive Committee. This is also extremely fool-hardy on the part of the PMI Leader.

There are instances where the Project Managers spent as much as 25% of their time preparing report components for presentation to the Executive Committee by the PMO Leadership. This represent a significant drain on the Project Managers ability to effectively manage projects.

** Correction **

A streamlined reporting process must be implemented from the outset. Ultimately, it is the responsibility of the Project Managers to manage the projects while the PMO Leadership is responsible for accurately reporting the health and status of the projects under its purview to the Executive Committee.

If the presentation decks are so complex that the PMO Leadership requires a measurable percentage of the Project Managers' time for preparation, the presentation should be revisited, or the PMO Leadership must find a means to automate this function or allocate dedicated PMO staff for presentation preparation.

It is not the responsibility of the Project Managers to do the PMO Leader's work.

Are Projects Prioritized

Many projects are prioritized by the rule of 'who makes the most noise'.

It is not unusual for projects to be given high priority based on the power or prestige of the sponsor, with little thought given to the other projects that may have greater importance to the organization.

Project prioritization is often haphazard and capricious. The entire organization can be held hostage by poorly prioritized projects. Projects must be prioritized based on the cost/benefit to the company.

Without a standardized methodology for prioritizing projects, the PMO Organization will be the owner of chaos, unable to explain or justify why projects are being worked.

While it is obvious that prioritization efforts will focus on the cost/benefit ratio, there are other, often 'intangible' factors that must be taken into consideration.

** Correction **

Every project under the control of the PMO Leader must be fairly and accurately prioritized against all other projects in the demand stream. Even if projects are realistically prioritized, they should be continually reviewed against evolving needs of the organization.

It is not the responsibility of the PMO Leader to single-handedly prioritize the projects in the demand stream or backlog. However, it is the responsibility to discuss and negotiate with the Business Leaders to determine the priority of the projects and what level of resource allocations is necessary.

The approved and prioritized projects will be 'above the bar', while the prioritized, but unapproved projects will be 'below the bar', in reference to a simple spreadsheet method of tracking projects. (By prioritizing those projects 'below the bar', the PMO Leader has a tool in hand to negotiate for activation of a project in the event that resources become available.

The Executive team must approve the priorities assigned to projects, and honor that approval. If urgent business needs dictate changing the priorities, the Executive team must support that change and understand the impact on resources.

Some projects will take precedence simply due to their nature; legal or regulatory requirements, keeping the business operating, and employee relations are good examples.

The Executive Committee must approve the final prioritization and determine if projects 'below the bar' are worthy enough to authorize contract resources.

Ensure that the prioritization process is clear, consistent, and defensible.

Change Control Process

Does the PMO have an existing and functioning change control process? Without an official Change Control Process, the PMO Organization will fail.

Due to the nature of business, changes to projects are inevitable. Without an effective change control process, any incremental change will result in uncontrolled 'scope creep'.

Be aware that in most cases, scope creep components are not listed on any change control documentation, resulting in problems and 'mismatches' when the project is delivered

Since many changes may result in extended schedules or increased costs, a Change Control Board (CCB) should have oversight of ALL project changes.

If budget or schedule-changing project 'additions' are accepted without approval while the budget and schedule remain fixed and the additional work is added, this will ensure that the project will be over budget and beyond the schedule

Keep in mind that schedule changes have a direct effect on all 'downstream' project resources.

** Correction **

One of the first processes the PMO should establish is a Change Control Process. The Change Control Board (CCB) should meet regularly, so that all members can ensure they have time on their calendars for those meetings. However, the CCB must be able to work with the PMO and Project Managers to ensure that critical changes are implemented in a timely manner and not delayed by a meeting schedule.

The PMO Leadership should present the change requests to the CCB and report the results of CCB meeting to the executives. The individual Project Managers should report CCB results to the stakeholders of their respective projects.

While there may be a discretionary level that the Project Manager can act without CCB approval, any changes MUST be documented. Be aware that if a limit is set, the Project Manager may sub-divide changes into smaller components to fit the changes into the limit by submitting the smaller components as separate changes, rather than the entire change request.

The PMO must be kept aware of any change to a project, whether it requires CCB approval or not.

PMO Evaluation

Now that we've had a chance to review some of the criteria used to evaluate a PMO Organization, it is time to discuss HOW to evaluate a PMO.

My method for evaluating a PMO involves a two-layer approach; using the Macro Factors for a gross evaluation and incorporating the Micro Factors to develop a more precise rating.

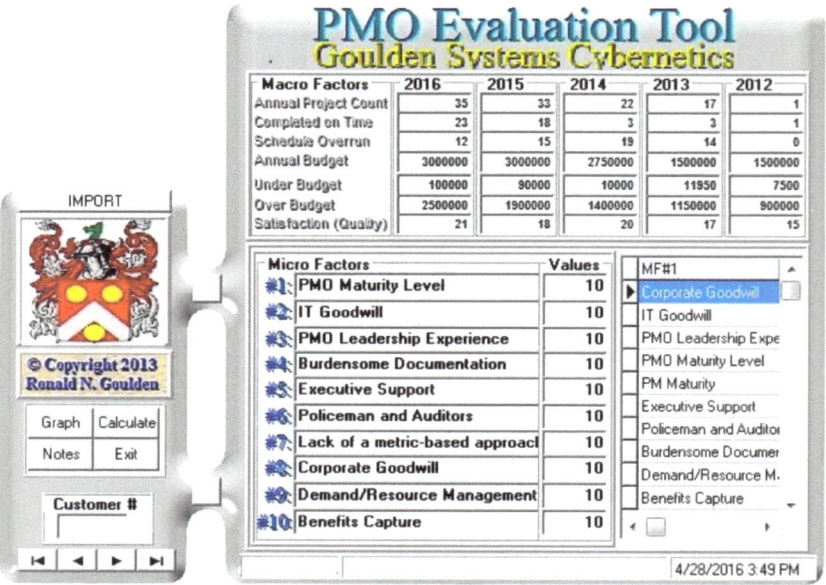

In looking at the preceding illustration, there are actually seven Macro Factor components to consider over the span of up to five years:

1. Annual Project Count – The number of projects assigned for each year provides a good year-over-year visual of how the Project Management function is growing (or diminishing). Of course the number of projects for each year is used as part of the evaluation calculations.

2. Projects Completed on Time – The year-over-year project completion number is a good indicator of the effectiveness of the Project Management processes. As long as the completion percentage (Completed/Total) for each year continues to improve, then the PMO is heading in the right direction.

3. Schedule Over-runs – The year-over-year project incompletion number is a good indicator of the failure of the Project Management processes. If this incompletion percentage (Schedule Overruns/Total) for each year continues to decline, then the PMO is heading in the wrong direction.

4. Annual Budget – As with the Annual Project Count, the Annual project Budget indicates how the Business views the PMO. If the year-over-year Project Budget increases, then the Business is indicating some level of confidence in the PMO. If the Project Budget declines year-over-year, then this could be a very bad sign for the PMO.

5. Under Budget – This is simply the annual aggregate comparison of total project expenditures to the budget for each year. If the aggregate is less than the budget then that year has an 'under budget' condition. This is generally a good sign, though there may be extenuating circumstances that might make this a less than joyous number.

6. Over Budget – This is simply the annual aggregate comparison of total project expenditures to the budget for each year. If the aggregate is more than the budget then that year has an 'over budget' condition. As with the 'under budget' condition, there may be extenuating circumstances that could make this a less onerous metric.

7. Satisfaction (Quality) – Finally, the year-over-year satisfaction index is the aggregate of each year's customer/project satisfaction surveys. Typically, the higher this number is, the better. A high or increasing satisfaction metric is generally a good sign.

When we start to discuss the Micro Factors, it is too burdensome to have the executives rate the PMO on all twenty Micro Factors. Typically, the executive committee and possibly the customer base, will agree on ten of the most relevant Micro factors and provide a value between zero (0) and ten (10), with ten being perfect.

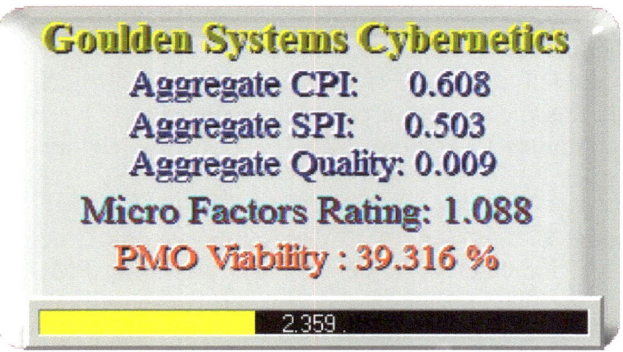

When the data has been provided and the calculations are completed, a simple graphic can be provided which provides six critical informational elements concerning eh PMO performance.

1. Aggregate CPI – As with the generally accepted scale for CPI, an aggregate CPI of 1 indicates that the PMO Cost performance is on budget. If the Aggregate CPI is greater than 1, then the PMO Cost performance is under budget. If the Aggregate CPI is less than 1 then the PMO project cost is over budget.

2. Aggregate SPI – As with the generally accepted scale for SPI, an aggregate SPI of 1 indicates that the PMO Schedule performance is on track. If the Aggregate SPI is greater than 1, then the PMO projects performance is ahead of schedule. If the Aggregate SPI is less than 1 then the PMO project performance is behind schedule.

3. Aggregate Quality – Ideally, the Aggregate Quality should be 1.000 (perfect). Any number less than 1.000 leaves room for improvement. The farther the Quality rating is from 1.000 indicates that the users (customers) are NOT satisfied with the results of the projects. This may be a result of the projects not providing the expected or desired results; or the projects were delivered so far behind schedule or over budget to be of little value to the customer

4. Micro Factors Rating – This is the result of a complicated calculation that essentially results in an aggregate value for all of the Micro Factors submitted. Typically, anything above 1.000 is considered acceptable. The primary purpose for this value is in calculating the PMO Viability and Overall Rating.

5. PMO Viability – PMO Viability is expressed as a simple percentage. 100% is perfect, Zero percent is horrible. A marginal PMO would be in the 60 to 70% range.

6. Overall Rating – The Overall Rating uses a different set of calculations and is based on a 0.000 to 8.000 scale, with 8.000 being the best 'World Class' rating. The coloration of the graph is the typical Red-Yellow-Green scale. Less than 2.000 is Red (fail). 2.001 to 4.999 is Yellow (average). Green (good) is any rating greater than or equal to 5.000.

Ultimately, it is the responsibility of the PMO Leader to ensure that the Project Management Office is functioning as expected by the Executive committee.

While the PMO Organization may be functioning perfectly, if the Executives do not see this, then the PMO Leader has failed the organization and the Business.

In times of financial or economic stress, the Business Executives have a responsibility to ensure that the Business if running as effectively as possible. This may mandate downsizing or outright elimination of functions that are perceived as a 'money pit' that does not provide a reasonable ROI to the Business. If the PMO is viewed as ineffective, then it is likely to be removed from the organization entirely.

Therefore, it is incumbent upon the PMO Leader to ensure that ALL levels of the Business are aware of what the PMO is doing and how it is adding value to the Business. The PMO Leader must advertise successes and mitigate failures while continually growing and perfecting its delivery processes.

With this single, simple graphic, the PMO Leader can comfortably express the status of the PMO Organization and the Project Management function in general.

###

Additional works by Ronald N. Goulden
http://www.rongoulden.com/Literary.htm

	Project Management for a Functional World
	https://www.createspace.com/3421657
	Learn Excel with the Quality Scorecard
	https://www.createspace.com/3428846
	Learn Excel: Executive Summary & Scope
	https://www.createspace.com/3718607
	Agile & Quality by Design
	https://www.createspace.com/5489597

www.ingramcontent.com/pod-product-compliance
Lightning Source LLC
Chambersburg PA
CBHW040929180526
45159CB00002BA/666